THE ESSENTIAL BOOK OF

Household
SPELLS AND

Magic

Beatrice Aurelia Crowley

Erebus Society

Erebus Society

First published in Great Britain in 2025
Erebus Society

First Edition

ISBN: 978-1-912461-72-1

www.ErebusSociety.com

Table of Contens

What is Household Magic?

One's home transcends mere walls and a roof; it serves as a sanctuary, a temple, and a holy location where energy circulates and enchantment integrates into the essence of daily existence. Household magic is the practice of converting one's residence into a sanctuary of safety, balance, abundance, and spiritual strength. This ancient practice imbues daily activities with purpose, vitality, and allure, transforming the ordinary into the extraordinary and the domestic into the sublime.

Household magic, shown by a strategically positioned broom and protective sigils above doorways, is intricately integrated into the traditions of hearth, home, and familial life. It is present in kitchen witchcraft, ancestor offerings, herbal safeguards, and daily rituals that protect and sanctify the home.

What, in essence, is household magic? What is its function, and what significance does it hold for the well-being, vitality, and safety of its inhabitants? Let us examine this revered craft along with its origins, methods, and influence in daily life.

ORIGINS AND HISTORY OF HOUSEHOLD MAGIC

Household magic has been practiced for millennia, transmitted through generations as folk lore, beliefs, and sacred traditions. Throughout societies, the home has consistently been perceived as a locus of power, where spirits dwell, ancestors oversee, and protective magic is most potent.

Ancient Civilisations and Household Magic

In Ancient Egypt, the Egyptians adorned their homes with protective amulets and hieroglyphic charms to repel malevolent spirits. Statues of Bes, the domestic guardian deity, were positioned near entrances to ward off disaster.

In ancient Rome and Greece, the Greeks and Romans revered Hestia (Vesta), the goddess of the hearth, and conducted daily fire rites to sanctify the home. Protective home deities (lares and penates) were honoured with offerings of food and incense.

The Celts regarded the home as a holy realm inhabited by ancestors. Witch's ladders, charms, and herbal sachets were strategically positioned throughout the residence for protection, while hearth fires were maintained to invite wealth.

The Norse erected runestones and inscribed sigils adjacent to doorways and windows to safeguard against roaming spirits and misfortune. Household ghosts referred to as Landvaettir were venerated to secure favourable fortune.

Medieval and Folk Traditions

In the mediaeval period, domestic magic became profoundly connected with folk traditions and superstition. Individuals suspended iron horseshoes above doorways to repel malevolence, interred witch bottles containing protecting objects beneath their residences, and inscribed lintels with sacred symbols to avert danger. Knowledgeable ladies and astute individuals offered herbal medicines, talismans, and domestic blessings to promote health and well-being in the household.

Modern Household Magic

Currently, domestic magic persists in kitchen witchcraft, energy purification, protective symbols, and the intentional placement of sacred items. The practice of domestic magic, utilising herbal sachets, enchanted candles, or daily spiritual cleansing, enables individuals to cultivate a home imbued with love, protection, and positive energy.

Understanding Household Magic

Household magic involves the utilisation of spells, charms, and rituals to sustain a tranquil, safeguarded, and spiritually enriched residence. It includes a diverse array of magical disciplines, such as:

❁ Protective Magic — Repelling adverse energy, entities, and misfortune.

❁ Prosperity and Abundance Magic - Attracting money, success, and good fortune into one's residence.

❁ Love and Harmony Magic — Fostering robust relationships, self-acceptance, and emotional equilibrium within the home.

❁ Purification and purification Magic - Eliminating sluggish or detrimental energy by spiritual purification.

❁ Kitchen and Hearth Magic — Employing food, herbs, and fire to sanctify and sustain the inhabitants.

Household magic operates by imbuing routine activities with purpose and spiritual vitality, transforming cooking, cleaning, decorating, and arranging into acts of enchantment.

Methods of Household Magic

1. Protective Household Amulets and Talismans

Applying salt lines at entrances and windows to repel negativity. Suspending iron horseshoes or protective symbols above doors. Employing witch bottles containing herbs, nails, and protective symbols interred in proximity to the residence.

2. Energy Purification and Benedictions

Utilise smoke cleansing with rosemary, cedar, or lavender to eliminate stagnant energy.

Dispersing consecrated water or lunar water in the corners of rooms.

Utilising bells or chimes to alter energy and dispel negativity.

3. Culinary and Hearth Enchantment

Incorporating intents into food during preparation (clockwise for blessings, anticlockwise for exile).

Utilising herbs such as cinnamon (prosperity), basil (love), and rosemary (protection) in baking.

Positioning a lit candle adjacent to the stove as an emblem of warmth and prosperity.

4. Residential Sanctification Rituals

Utilising a besom to cleanse the home of negative energy.

Positioning rose quartz or amethyst in the bedroom to foster affection and facilitate restorative sleep.

Inscribing sigils on doors and windowsills for spiritual safeguarding.

5. Altars and Sacred Areas

Establishing a domestic altar with offerings to ancestors, spirits, or deities for safeguarding purposes.

Utilising crystals, candles, and incense to maintain positive energy flow.

Honouring the four elements (earth, air, fire, water) by integrating natural symbols within the residence.

Magical Correspondences

These herbs and crystals can be used in household charms, protective wards, cleansing rituals, and home blessings to create a sacred and harmonious living space.

HERBS

BASIL

Attracts prosperity, love, and peace; wards off negative energy in the home.

BAY LEAF

Used for protection, prosperity, and wish magic; often placed in doorways or burned for purification.

CATNIP

Encourages harmony and relaxation in the home; strengthens bonds between household members.

CEDAR

A powerful herb for protection and energy cleansing; burned as incense to purify a home.

CHAMOMILE

Brings peace, calm, and financial luck; used in home blessings and floor washes.

CINNAMON

Attracts prosperity, warmth, and loving energy; used in kitchen magic and home protection spells.

CLOVE

Provides protection and removes negativity; often used in charm bags and warding spells.

ELDERFLOWER

Enhances spiritual protection and strengthens connections with household spirits.

EUCALYPTUS

Clears stagnant energy, repels negativity, and promotes health within the home.

GARLIC

Wards off negative entities, illness, and bad energy; placed near doors for protection.

GINGER

Adds warmth and vitality to the home; encourages motivation and success.

HONEYSUCKLE

Attracts prosperity and sweetens the energy within a household.

JUNIPER

Purifies the home and protects against harmful spirits; often burned as incense.

LAVENDER

Brings peace, relaxation, and a sense of love; placed under pillows for restful sleep.

LEMON BALM

Encourages joy, healing, and emotional balance within the home.

MINT

Refreshes energy, promotes clarity, and attracts good luck and prosperity.

ROSEMARY

One of the most powerful herbs for household protection and purification; used in floor washes and smoke cleansing.

SAGE

(Common Garden Sage)

Purifies and protects the home, dispelling negative energy.

THYME

Enhances courage and dispels bad luck; used in home blessings and spiritual cleansing.

VANILLA

Fosters warmth, comfort, and emotional well-being in the home.

CRYSTALS AND MINERALS

AMETHYST
Provides spiritual protection, calming energy, and dream clarity; often placed in bedrooms.

BLACK TOURMALINE
Shields the home from negativity, psychic attacks, and unwanted energy.

CARNELIAN
Promotes warmth, joy, and vitality within a household.

CELESTITE
Encourages peace, angelic guidance, and harmonious energy.

CITRINE
Attracts prosperity, abundance, and happiness to a home.

CLEAR QUARTZ
Amplifies positive energy, purifies spaces, and enhances spiritual work.

FLUORITE
Helps maintain order, clarity, and balance within a household.

GARNET
Strengthens bonds within family and promotes warmth and stability.

HEMATITE
Grounds energy, provides strong protection, and stabilises the home's energy field.

JADE
Brings prosperity, harmony, and a sense of peace to the home.

LABRADORITE
Protects against unwanted influences and enhances the home's magical energy.

LAPIS LAZULI
Encourages honesty, wisdom, and strong communication within the household.

MALACHITE
Absorbs negative energy and promotes transformation and renewal.

MOONSTONE
Enhances intuition, emotional balance, and peaceful energy in the home.

OBSIDIAN
(Black or Snowflake)

Provides deep protection and clears negativity from living spaces.

PYRITE
Brings prosperity and financial stability to the home.

ROSE QUARTZ
Fosters love, harmony, and emotional well-being in relationships.

SELENITE

Cleanses energy, promotes serenity, and strengthens the spiritual atmosphere.

SMOKY QUARTZ

Grounds energy, removes negativity, and promotes a stable environment.

TIGER'S EYE

Brings courage, protection, and prosperity to the home.

Tips for a Magical and Harmonious Living Space

Welcome to the captivating realm of witchcraft, where commonplace objects and straightforward ceremonies can convert your residence into a haven of enchantment and tranquilly. Regardless of your level of expertise in witchcraft, these domestic suggestions will assist you in establishing an environment that emanates positivity, safety, and serenity.

PROTECTIVE SALT BARRIER

For millennia, salt has been utilised in magical activities due to its protecting attributes. To repel negativity, distribute a line of salt over thresholds, windowsills, and the perimeter of your residence. This imperceptible barrier prevents the intrusion of undesirable energies and spirits.

Tip: For an added boost, mix the salt with dried rosemary and lavender.

BROOM CLEANSING RITUAL

Use a broom to sweep away negative energy in addition to cleaning. Before dawn, sweep your house from the rear to the front door with a broom made of natural materials or a besom.

As you sweep, chant:

> "With this broom, I sweep away
> All negativity, clear the way.
> Peace and harmony now reside,
> Within these walls, let love abide."

HERB SACHETS FOR PROTECTION AND LUCK

Make little sachets using herbs that are protective, such as lavender, rosemary, and dill, sew the herbs into tiny squares of fabric, and store them in closets, drawers, or beneath pillows. These sachets not only keep bad things away from your home, but they also bring luck and peace.

BLESSED WATER FOR CLEANSING

Create a magical water mixture to purify and cleanse your house. Steep rosemary, bay leaves, and dried marjoram in water that is nearly boiling. Let it cool, sieve the herbs, and scatter the infusion throughout your house while chanting:

> "I banish evil and negativity,
> This is my will, blessed be."

MAGICAL HOUSE GUARDIANS

Invite protective spirits into your home with symbolic representations such as statues, pictures, or crafted items. Place these guardians near doors and windows, and light a white candle while saying:

> "Guardians of home, strong and true,
> Protect this space in all we do."

MIRROR MAGIC FOR PROTECTION

Mirrors have the ability to reflect negative energy out of your house. Place tiny, outward-facing mirrors close to entryways. This will assist in diverting any malicious intent that may be aimed at your house.

Tip: Enchant the mirrors by anointing their edges with protective oils like frankincense or sandalwood.

LUNAR CLEANSING RITUAL

Perform home cleansing rituals in conjunction with the moon phases. Concentrate on chasing negativity away during the waning moon. Light a sage smudge stick and walk through each room, directing the smoke into corners and saying:

> *"As the moon wanes, negativity flees,*
> *Cleansed and pure, my home shall be."*

CANDLE MAGIC FOR PEACE

To promote harmony and peace, light candles. Use white or blue candles that have been anointed with peace oil, which is a mixture of rose, chamomile, and lavender. As you meditate on peace permeating every room of your house, place them in the middle and let them burn for an hour.

CRYSTAL GRIDS FOR ENERGY BALANCE

To balance the energy in your house, arrange crystals in a grid. Use stones such as citrine for good vibes, amethyst for peace, and black tourmaline for protection. Position the grid in the middle of your house and picture the crystals' energies spreading outward.

Tip: Cleanse the crystals regularly by placing them under moonlight or in a bowl of saltwater.

ENCHANTED PLANTS FOR SPIRITUAL PURITY

Include spiritually beneficial houseplants, such as aloe vera, which guards against negativity, peace lilies, which encourage harmonic energy, and rosemary, which purifies. Put these plants in strategic locations and speak to them, bringing your intentions to life.

Tip: Keep a small garden of magical herbs like sage, thyme, and basil, which can be used in various spells and rituals.

USE ESSENTIAL OILS FOR ENERGY CLEANSING

To purify the energy in your house, diffuse essential oils such as rosemary, frankincense, or lavender. Because of their cleansing qualities, these oils can aid in removing negativity and fostering a peaceful environment.

Tip: Place a few drops of essential oil on cotton balls and tuck them into corners or hidden spots around your home for continuous cleansing.

CREATE AN ALTAR

In a peaceful area in your house, erect a little altar. Add objects that symbolise the four elements: a bowl of water for water, a candle for fire, a plant or stone for earth, and feathers or incense for air. This hallowed area can be used as a centre for introspection and meditation.

DECORATE WITH SYMBOLIC ART

Display artwork that exudes protection and good vibes. Your house can be blessed and protected by symbols such as the evil eye, pentacles, or pictures of gods. Select artwork that inspires you and supports your goals.

INCORPORATE FENG SHUI PRINCIPLES

To balance the flow of energy in your house, implement fundamental Feng Shui principles. Use mirrors to increase light and energy, arrange furniture to promote a smooth flow of chi, and clear clutter. Make sure your entrance is open and unhindered.

USE SOUND FOR ENERGY CLEARING

Regularly employ music to cleanse stagnant energy. You can ring a bell, play a singing bowl, or simply clap your hands in the corners of each room. The vibrations from the sound aid to break up and remove negative energy.

PLACE PROTECTIVE CRYSTALS

Place protective crystals strategically throughout your home. Amethyst in living areas encourages calm, black tourmaline near entryways helps protect against negative energy, and clear quartz can enhance the positive energy in your house.

Tip: Cleanse your crystals regularly by placing them in sunlight or moonlight.

MAINTAIN A CLEAN AND ORGANIZED SPACE

A clean and organized home naturally attracts positive energy. Regularly clear up, dust, and declutter to ensure the energy in your home flows easily. Peace and order are fostered by a clean home.

UTILIZE MOON WATER

Overnight, place a bowl of water in the moonlight to create moon water. Use this water to add to your plants, anoint windows and doors, and clean surfaces. Your home's spiritual atmosphere will be enhanced with moon water, which is charged with lunar energy.

Tip: Different phases of the moon impart different energies; choose the phase that aligns with your intentions.

CREATE A PROTECTIVE GARDEN

Use plants and herbs with magical qualities to create a protecting garden. Sage, lavender, and rosemary are great options for purification and protection. In addition to adding vitality to your house, a garden supplies the materials for magical processes.

Houseplants to Purify Your Living Space, Spiritually and Physically

As a witch, you know that genuine magic originates in the natural world. Taking care of houseplants improves your health and well-being while also deepening your connection to nature. In addition to bringing their own magical energies into your house, these five enchanted plants purify the air by eliminating chemical vapours from paints, cleaners, and solvents.

ALOE VERA

Aloe Vera, well-known for its therapeutic qualities, also protects against negative energy and ill luck. To keep your house safe, put it in your kitchen or close to entrances.

ARECA PALM
(Butterfly or Yellow Palm)

The Areca Palm infuses your room with tranquilly and inspires creativity. Its elegant fronds flourish in indirect, brilliant light, bringing inspiration and peace to your house.

BOSTON FERN

This rich fern is a potent ally for improving intuition and psychic powers. To make sure its magical qualities are at their best, keep it in a humid environment.

ENGLISH IVY

English Ivy is particularly nice for newlyweds since it brings good fortune and security. It is easy to maintain while it performs its magic because it can grow in a variety of light situations.

GERBERA DAISY

These colourful flowers are ideal for elevating moods and promoting joy. To make your house and your attitude happier, put them in areas that receive plenty of sunlight.

JASMINE

Attracts money and affection. The aromatic blossoms of jasmine are a potent way to attract good energy associated with love, wealth, and spiritual development.

LAVENDER

Promotes relaxation and peace. Lavender is great for bedrooms to guarantee restful sleep and pleasant dreams, while its aroma purifies the air and raises the spirit.

PEACE LILY

The Peace Lily is well known for enhancing communication and promoting pleasant vibes. It is a flexible addition to any space because it grows well in shaded spots.

ROSEMARY

Increases focus and memory while offering protection. To improve mental clarity and ward off negative energy, put rosemary at your workspace or study.

SNAKE PLANT
(Mother-in-Law's Tongue)

Provides powerful defence against negative energy and nasty vibes. This resilient plant is great for enhancing air quality and protecting the house.

Tips:

Bond with Your Plants: Speak to them, touch their leaves gently, and let them know they are loved. This strengthens the magical connection.

17

Placement:

Position your plants in places where they can thrive physically and spiritually, such as near windows for light-loving species or in quiet corners for those that prefer shade.

Care:

Regularly water, feed, and prune your plants. Healthy plants are more potent in their magical and purifying abilities.

Spells

Angelic Banishing Spell for Unwanted Spirits

REQUIREMENTS:

❀ Sage incense
❀ White candles
❀ A glass of water
❀ Sacred jewelry

INSTRUCTIONS:

Light the sage incense and white candles, creating a sacred and pure atmosphere.

Wear your sacred jewelry to enhance your connection to protective energies.

Invocation:

Stand tall, feeling the power and strength within you.

Shout this mantra with conviction:

Guardians of light, come swiftly, draw near,
Cleanse this space of spirits, who should not be here!
Heavenly protectors, with wings so bright,
Banish all shadows, restore peace tonight.
Divine sentinels, hear my earnest plea,
Guide away all forces that disturb harmony.
Celestial beings, with power so grand,
Clear away all entities, by your gentle hand.
Holy defenders, with grace you endear,
Sweep away all presences, that do not belong here.

Blessed guardians, with purity and might,
Dispel all dark spirits, into the night.
Sacred protectors, with light so clear,
Shield this place from those, who should not be near.
Angelic forces, with compassion and care,
Remove all spirits, and purify the air.

Call upon your highest teacher, angel, or deity to assist in clearing the spirit from your space.

Visualize their powerful presence surrounding you, providing guidance and protection.

Hold the glass of water in your hands, infusing it with the intention to absorb negativity.

Place it in the center of the room or the affected area, allowing it to draw in unwanted energies.

Meditate in the newly cleansed space, visualizing the atmosphere around you being purified.

Feel the presence of protective angels guarding your space, banishing all evil spirits.

After meditation, flush the water down the drain, symbolizing the removal of all negativity.

Express gratitude to the angels and higher powers for their assistance.

Extinguish the candles and incense, sealing the banishing spell.

Attract Visitors to a Home

REQUIREMENTS:

✺ Fresh or dried basil leaves

INSTRUCTIONS:

Gather fresh or dried basil leaves, known for their protective and welcoming properties.

Using a mortar and pestle, grind the basil leaves into a fine powder, focusing your intention on creating a space that welcomes kind and friendly visitors.

Stand at the main entrance of your home, holding the basil powder in your hands.

Close your eyes and envision a warm, glowing light surrounding your home, a beacon for good-hearted guests.

As you sprinkle the basil powder around the entrance, chant with belief:

> "Basil blessed, guard this door,
> Draw kind souls forevermore.
> Friends and joy, come to me,
> Harmful hearts, away shall flee."

Imagine the basil powder forming an invisible shield, a protective barrier that only allows those with pure intentions to enter.

Stand quietly for a moment, feeling the energy of your spell solidify and spread throughout your home.

Trust in the magic you have cast, knowing your home is now a haven for friendly and positive visitors.

Attraction to Sell a House

REQUIREMENTS:

❀ Green candle
❀ Cinnamon incense, potpourri, or lamp ring

INSTRUCTIONS:

Mundane Work:

List the house with a reputable agent.

Clean the house thoroughly.

Place a "For Sale" sign outside.

Advertise in the newspaper.

Inform everyone that the house is for sale.

Ritual:

Find a quiet time when the street is least busy.

Stand or sit in a spot where you can see the house clearly without disturbance.

Face the house from the same perspective a potential buyer would have.

Hold the green candle and close your eyes.

Take deep breaths to relax and focus.

Enter a meditative state.

23

Picture the house in brilliant sunlight, glowing and inviting.

Walk through the house in your mind, seeing it as a potential buyer would.

Imagine every feature of the house at its best: clean, bright, and welcoming.

Envision the plants thriving and the rooms filled with light.

As you mentally walk through the house, gather the light energy in each room.

Let this energy flow into you, then into the candle.

Spend a moment in each room to absorb the light.

Mentally exit the house, still absorbing the light.

Stand in the driveway, seeing the house bathed in light.

Transfer this energy from the house, through you, into the candle.

Sit or stand with your eyes closed for a moment.

Let any excess energy flow naturally into the ground.

Open your eyes.

Light the candle at a strategic time, such as the night before a showing.

Choose an auspicious moment: full moon for abundance, first quarter moon for new beginnings, Monday (day of the moon), or Thursday (day of Jupiter).

As you light the candle, say:

"Energy fill this home of mine,
Prosperity will now align.
Light and beauty, all around,
New owners soon shall be found."

Let the candle burn down completely.

Before each showing, subtly scent the house with cinnamon to evoke a sense of home and prosperity.

Call Upon The House Guardians

REQUIREMENTS:

❀ Representations of guardians for each door
(pictures, statues, crafts, etc.)
❀ Cleansed white candle for each guardian
❀ Sage smudge stick or cleansing incense (sandalwood or raw sage)

INSTRUCTIONS:

Cleansing the Home

Begin at the front door with a smudge stick and a bowl to catch ashes.
Chant:

> "As I walk through every room,
> Clear this space of any gloom.
> Bar the windows, seal the door,
> Let negativity enter no more."

Light the smudge stick and say:

> "As I walk this house, may it be cleansed of all negativity."

Walk clockwise around the house, moving the smudge stick counter-clock-wise or in a straight line toward the walls, visualizing negative energy being pushed out.

When you reach a window, trace bars over it with the smudge stick and say:

> "I bar this portal from allowing anything to enter."

For outside doors, draw a circle around the doorframe three times and say:

"May no negative energies enter.
If a negative person enters, may they leave their negativity outside."

Finish back at the front door and say:

"This house is cleansed and pure."

Inviting the Guardians

Gather the guardian representations and candles where your family spends the most time (dining room table, etc.).

Set a candle before each representation.

Chant:

"Spirit of this house, come to me,
Guard this home and keep it free.
Protect us all, both day and night,
In your care, we find our light."

Light the first candle, thinking of the door it will guard, and say:

"I welcome a spirit of this house to guard and protect all who dwell here."

Repeat with other guardians as needed.

Meditate with the guardians, then place them in their designated positions and extinguish the candles.

Introducing the Family

Light the candles and call the guardians where you first called upon them.

Chant:

> "Guardians, meet those who dwell here,
> Protect them all, keep them near.
> Family and pets, all who reside,
> Under your watch, safely abide."

<u>Introduce each family member, including pets.</u>

If someone in the household does not wish to participate, inform the guardians to protect them as well.

<u>Maintaining the Connection</u>

Call the guardians as needed using the same method.

Meditate with them regularly by lighting the candles and inviting their presence.

On special occasions like May Day, do something extra for them.

Inform the guardians of any changes or new events in the house.

Leave small dishes of leftover food and drink from dinner for the guardians.

Place these offerings in a spot where pets and children cannot reach.

Chant:

"Guardians, thanks for all you do,
Here's our offering, pure and true.
Essence taken, protection we gain,
In our home, may you remain."

Charm for Household Protection

REQUIREMENTS:

❈ Three dried twigs of equal length
❈ A vine for binding
❈ One white candle
❈ Protection oil
❈ Incense for protection
(choose a scent like frankincense, sage, or sandalwood)

INSTRUCTIONS:

At dawn, venture out to find three dried twigs of the same length, small enough to be carried as a charm. Bind them together with the vine.

At home, place the bound twigs on a table, surrounded by a lit white candle anointed with protection oil.

Light the incense and allow its smoke to rise.

Hold the twigs and pass them through the incense smoke several times while chanting:

> "Smoke of incense, pure and true,
> Bless these twigs in protective hue.
> Shield me, guard me from all harm,
> Hold me safe within your charm."

Continue to pass the twigs through the smoke, visualizing a strong protective barrier forming around them.

Once done, place the twigs in a small pouch and keep it with you at all times. Alternatively, hang the charm on the threshold of your home to ward off any evil.

As you finish the ritual, say:

"Twigs bound tight and blessed with light,
Guard me well both day and night.
By the power of this charm I see,
My protection strong, so let it be!"

Chinese Magical House Wash

REQUIREMENTS:

❀ Essential oils of Oriental Grasses (citronella grass, lemongrass, ginger-
grass, palmarosa grass, khus khus grass, vetivert grass)
❀ Broomcorn straws (from a natural broom or broomcorn plants)
❀ Van Van oil concentrate
❀ A small lump of frankincense gum
❀ Liquid oil soap (e.g., Murphy's Oil Soap)
❀ Water for dilution

INSTRUCTIONS:

Gather your essential oils of Oriental Grasses: citronella grass, lemongrass, gingergrass, palmarosa grass, khus khus grass, and vetivert grass.
Use a combination or select your favorites.

Cut a bunch of broomcorn straws from a natural broom or broomcorn
plants. Place the straws in a clean bottle.

Add a generous squirt of Van Van oil concentrate into the bottle with the
broomcorn straws. Place a small lump of frankincense gum into the bottle
as well.

Pour your liquid oil soap (such as Murphy's Oil Soap) into the bottle,
filling it to the top.

Seal the bottle and shake it gently, blending all the ingredients together.
As you mix, envision your home being cleansed and protected, and chant:

"Grasses of the East, cleanse and renew,
Frankincense pure, guide me true.
Broomcorn straws, sweep away,
All that hinders night or day."

Before using, dilute your Magic Chinese House Wash in water.

Using the diluted mixture, wash the floors, walls, and surfaces of your home. As you clean, visualize negativity being swept away and replaced with positive energy. Chant:

"With this wash, I cleanse and clear,
Bringing peace and love near.
By the power of these sacred blends,
My home is blessed, where harmony mends."

Cleansing a New Home

REQUIREMENTS:

❀ Chinese Wash or Van Van Oil
❀ A brand new broom
❀ Van Van Powder (optional)
❀ Salt

INSTRUCTIONS:

Mix Chinese Wash or Van Van Oil with water.

Begin at the back of the house, washing down the woodwork and floors, moving from back to front.

As you finish washing each room, move towards the front door.

Throw the remaining wash water out the front door or into the front yard.

If there is no front yard, carry some of the wash water to the nearest street intersection or crossroads and throw it to the East.

Use a brand new broom to sweep the house from back to front, moving out the front door.

If you choose, sprinkle Van Van Powder at the front threshold and sweep it away from the house.

After cleaning, place pinches of salt in the corners of each room.

If pressed for time, place four pinches of salt at the four outside corners of the house.

As you cleanse and bless your home, recite the following words to invite positive energies and protect against unwanted spirits:

"By the waters cleansed and purified,
With sacred broom, all harm denied.
From back to front, this home is free,
Blessed and safe, in harmony.
With salt and wash, I cast away,
All that hinders night and day.
Spirits pure, within these walls,
Hear my call, protect us all."

Ensure the salt remains in the corners to continue the protective and purifying effect.

Feel the peace and positivity fill your home, knowing it is blessed and cleansed.

Disturbance Away

REQUIREMENTS:

✤ Freshly cut parsley
✤ A pan of water
✤ Dried valerian root
✤ Teapot
✤ Three cups of water

INSTRUCTIONS FOR OUTSIDE DISTURBANCES:

Gather freshly cut parsley from your garden or purchase fresh parsley from a store.

Place the parsley in a pan of water and let it soak for nine minutes.

As the parsley soaks, visualize a serene and harmonious environment within your home.

After nine minutes, sprinkle the parsley-infused water throughout the house while chanting:

> "With parsley's touch, I cast away,
> All discord that has come to stay.
> Peaceful winds now gently blow,
> Bringing calm and soothing flow."

INSTRUCTIONS FOR IN-HOUSE DISTURBANCES:

Heat three cups of water until it is just boiling.

Place three teaspoons of dried valerian root in a teapot.

Pour the hot water over the valerian root and let it steep for 13 minutes.

Strain the mixture and prepare to sprinkle it around your home.

As you sprinkle the valerian infusion, chant:

> "Valerian root, with power so bright,
> Banish strife, restore the light.
> Peace within these walls reside,
> Harmony and calm abide."

Move through each room, ensuring the valerian infusion touches every corner, visualising the negative energy dissipating and tranquility taking its place.

Enchanted Closet
OR
Drawer Herbal Sachets

Infuse your clothes with the essence of magical herbs, ensuring they remain safe from insects and imbued with a touch of nature's charm.

REQUIREMENTS:

❋ Handfuls of dried lavender flowers
❋ Handfuls of dried rosemary
❋ 1 tablespoon of crushed cloves
❋ Small pieces of dried lemon peel

INSTRUCTIONS:

Gather your dried lavender flowers, rosemary, crushed cloves, and dried lemon peel.

Mix them together in a bowl, allowing their magical properties to blend.

Cut small cotton squares, approximately four by four inches.

Sew the squares together, leaving a small opening for stuffing.

Fill each cotton square with the herb mixture.

Sew the opening shut, ensuring the herbs are securely inside.

Tie several sachets together using raffia.

Wrap the bundles in tissue paper for an extra touch of elegance.

Write a note explaining the purpose of these sachets:

"These enchanted sachets protect clothes from insects. Place them in drawers, closets, or boxes to infuse your garments with the magical essence of lavender, rosemary, cloves, and lemon peel."

Place the sachets in your desired locations, visualizing their protective energy enveloping your clothes.

End of Day Home Cleansing

REQUIREMENTS:

❈ Sagebrush stick
❈ Glass of water
❈ Bowl with a shallow pool of water

INSTRUCTIONS:

Perform this spell preferably during a waning moon, but it can be cast at any time. Any evening after sunset will work.

Light the end of the sagebrush stick. Have a glass of water and a bowl containing a shallow pool of water nearby.

Blow out the flame and gently blow on the embers to increase the smoke.

In each room of your house, blow smoke in each of the four directions, gently blowing upon the burning stick as you face each wall of the room.

As you do this, say aloud:

> "From this space, negativity departs,
> All energy that does not belong,
> Return to your source, be gone, be strong."

When you are done with your whole house, return to the room you started in.

Take the stick and dip it into the shallow bowl of water to douse the embers.

Take a sip of water from your glass and say aloud:

"May this home be calm and bright,
Filled with peace, both day and night.
Grateful thanks, our wish is sealed,
Harmony and joy revealed."

Find Your Ideal Apartment or House

REQUIREMENTS:

❧ 1 green candle
❧ 1 gold candle
❧ Incense of cinnamon and patchouli
❧ Ads of apartments or homes

Timing:

Best performed during a Waxing Moon or Full Moon, preferably on a Sunday.

INSTRUCTIONS:

Gather ads from newspapers or rental books that showcase the type of apartment or house you desire.

Place these ads on your altar.

Place the green candle and gold candle on either side of the ads.

Light the incense of cinnamon and patchouli to fill the space with a fragrant aura.

Light the green candle, symbolizing the earth and your new home.

Light the gold candle, symbolizing the money needed and success in your quest.

As the candles burn, focus on the image of your perfect home and chant:

> "Element of Fire, with your light so bright,
> Illuminate the path to my new home tonight.
> Show me the place where I'll reside,
> A haven of peace where dreams abide."

Allow the candles to burn down completely.

Herbal Protection Sachet

REQUIREMENTS:

❂ 7″ square of cotton
❂ Basil
❂ Fennel
❂ Dill
❂ Red string

INSTRUCTIONS:

Place the basil, fennel, and dill in the center of the cotton cloth.

Gather the cloth and tie it up with the red string.

With the first knot, chant:

"I bind you to guard this home, and all who dwell within."

Tie a total of **13** knots, repeating the chant with each knot.

Pick up your Athame with your prominent hand.

Face the North, and gently poke the sachet with the tip of the Athame, saying:

"This charm I've crafted with my own hands, will serve as guardian of this home and all within its walls. Protector and sentinel, from now on."

Hang the sachet in the highest part of your home.

Conclude with the affirmation:

"It is done."

Home-Blessing Bread

REQUIREMENTS:

❊ A loaf of bread
❊ A pinch of salt
❊ Purifying or protecting incense
(such as frankincense, cinnamon, or pepper)
❊ An incense burner

INSTRUCTIONS:

Begin by offering a piece of bread to the household guardians. Place the bread in a special place as a sign of respect and gratitude.

Take a pinch of salt and place it in the heart of your home, where it will serve to ground any evil that might try to enter.

Light the purifying or protecting incense in the incense burner. Allow the fragrant smoke to rise, filling the air with its cleansing properties.

Start at the entrance of your home and slowly move from room to room, carrying the incense burner.

As you move through each room, visualize any negativity fleeing and being replaced by a protective and positive energy.

As you move through your home, chant the following words of power, letting their energy cleanse and bless your space:

"Smoke of air and fire and earth,
Cleanse and bless this home and hearth.
Drive away all harm and fear,
Only good may dwell in here."

Once you have moved through each room, return to the heart of your home.

Place the incense burner in a safe location and allow it to burn out completely.

Stand for a moment, feeling the purified and blessed energy that now fills your home.

44

Honor Household Spirits

REQUIREMENTS:

❈ Incense of your choice
❈ Candles
❈ Offerings (such as small foods, flowers, or special items)

INSTRUCTIONS:

Set up a small altar or sacred space in your home.

Place the incense and candles on the altar.

Arrange the offerings you have chosen for your household spirits.

Light the incense, allowing its fragrant smoke to fill the space.

Light the candles, creating a warm and inviting atmosphere.

Stand before your altar, focusing your intentions on honoring the spirits that reside within your home.

Recite the following chant with reverence and sincerity:

> "Spirits of this house, take heart and thrive,
> In every chamber, let light arrive.
> To every corner, this breath I send,
> Approve my gifts, and be my friend."

Gently place your offerings on the altar, letting the spirits know these gifts are for them.

Feel the connection grow between you and the household spirits, inviting their protection and favor.

Allow the incense and candles to burn for as long as you feel necessary.

When ready, extinguish the candles and thank the spirits for their presence and protection.

House Bottle Against Harm

REQUIREMENTS:

❀ A small jar with a cap or cork
❀ Pins and needles
❀ Fresh rosemary sprigs
❀ Red wine
❀ A black or red candle

INSTRUCTIONS:

Hold each ingredient in your hand, focusing on its protective properties.

As you add each ingredient to the jar, say:

"Pins, needles, rosemary, wine,
In this witch's bottle of mine.
Guard against harm and enmity,
This is my will, so shall it be!"

Visualize the pins and needles piercing through negativity, the rosemary sending away all harm, and the wine drowning any evil forces.

Fill the jar with red wine, imagining it purifying and protecting your space.

Seal the jar tightly with the cap or cork, then drip wax from the black or red candle around the seal to secure it.

Bury the jar at the farthest corner of your property or place it in a hidden spot within your home.

Chant:

Pins and needles, sharp and fine,
In this bottle, protection combine.
Rosemary strong, send harm away,
With red wine, let evil sway.
Guard this space from all that's vile,
Within this jar, darkness exile.
My will is strong, this spell is cast,
Protection here, now and last.

House Protection Jar

REQUIREMENTS:

❂ 1 glass bottle or jar with a cap
❂ Mixing bowl
❂ Funnel (can be made with a rolled-up piece of paper)
❂ 9 herbs of choice from the following list:

Acacia, Aloe, Angelica, Anise, Ash, Basil, Birch, Blackberry, Blueberry, Broom, Caraway, Carnation, Cedar, Cinquefoil, Clover, Cotton, Cypress, Dill, Eucalyptus, Fennel, Flax, Foxglove, Grass, Hazel, Heather, Holly, Irish Moss, Ivy, Lilac, Mandrake, Marigold, Mistletoe, Mugwort, Mulberry, Oak, Olive, Pine, Primrose, Raspberry, Rice, Rose, Rosemary, Sandalwood, Spanish Moss, Thistle, Valerian, Violet, Willow

INSTRUCTIONS:

Find a quiet place where you can work undisturbed.

Arrange your tools and ingredients before you.

One by one, add each of the nine selected herbs into the mixing bowl. As you pour each herb, say:

"_____, that protects, guard my home and all within."

Use your hands to mix the herbs, focusing on the intent of safeguarding your home. Envision a strong barrier of protection surrounding your dwelling.

Use the funnel to transfer the mixed herbs into the glass bottle or jar. As you do this, continue to visualize your home being shielded from harm.

Cap the bottle or jar securely. Hold it in your hands and infuse it with your protective energy.

If you can, bury the bottle outside, in front of your front step. If this is not possible, hide the jar somewhere discreet but near your doorway.

When you place the bottle, chant:

> "By earth and herb, this charm is cast,
> Protection strong, this spell shall last.
> Home secure from ill and plight,
> Guard us well, day and night."

Household Blessing

REQUIREMENTS:

❋ Incense for purification (such as sage or sandalwood)
❋ A white candle
❋ A small bowl of salt
❋ A small bowl of water
❋ A feather for air
❋ A small stone for earth

INSTRUCTIONS:

Cleanse your space with the incense, allowing the smoke to drift through each room.

Light the white candle to invoke purity and protection.

Place the bowl of salt and water, the feather, and the stone in a circle around the candle.

Stand in the center of your home, holding the candle, and recite:

"Home of stone, metal, wood, and earth,
Protected by spirits since its birth.
From the four winds, guard this space,
Fill it with joy, love, and grace.
Keeper of health, wealth, and peace,
May all troubles now cease.
Dwelling strong and dwelling fair,
Shielded by magic, free from care.
Pure and clean this space shall be,
In perfect love and harmony.
Secure and calm, your peace shall last,

All dark energies now be cast.
Finished in beauty, this spell is true,
Blessings abound, from me to you.
Finished in beauty, my work is done,
This home is blessed by moon and sun."

Dip your fingers in the salt water and sprinkle it lightly around each room, visualizing a protective barrier forming.

Place the stone at your front door as a guardian, and let the candle burn down safely to complete the spell. As you finish, say:

"In this home,
peace shall dwell,
Guarded by magic,
all is well."

Lucky Home

REQUIREMENTS:

❀ A small package of dried alfalfa

INSTRUCTIONS:

Begin by holding the package of dried alfalfa in your hands.

Close your eyes and visualize your home filled with vibrant, positive energy and good fortune.

As you focus on this visualization, chant the following incantation to charge the alfalfa with your intent:

"Alfalfa green, luck's embrace,
Fill this home with fortune's grace.
Bless this space with charm and cheer,
Good luck abound, year after year."

Open your eyes and walk to your kitchen or pantry.

Place the charged alfalfa package in a cupboard, preferably one that you use often, to ensure that the luck is spread throughout your home.

After placing the alfalfa, hold your hands over the cupboard door and say:

"With alfalfa here, luck will stay,
Bless this home in every way.
By my will and magic bright,
Good fortune now is in my sight."

Close the cupboard door, knowing that your home is now blessed with the positive energy and luck of the alfalfa.

Feel the warmth and protection of the spell enveloping your living space.

Magic Broom Home Cleansing

Requirements:

- A broom, preferably one dedicated to magical use

Instructions:

Stand in the center of the room you wish to cleanse.

Hold your broom firmly, feeling its connection to your will and power.

Begin sweeping the room in a deosil (clockwise) direction.

As you sweep, recite the following incantation:

"With this broom, tool of my might,
I cleanse and purify this sacred site.
From this circle, fear I expel,
Malice and misfortune, I dispel.
May this space be pure and bright,
A meeting place of divine light.
Gods and spirits, hear my plea,
This space is cleansed, so mote it be."

As you sweep, visualize the broom gathering all negative energy, fear, and malice.

Imagine these negative forces being drawn into the broom, leaving the space clear and bright.

Once you have swept the entire room, step outside and shake the broom to release the gathered negativity away from your home.

Return to the room and feel the newfound peace and purity within the space.

Magic Water of Home Tranquility

Add this enchanted water to your scrub water to cleanse your home, promoting peace and calm.

REQUIREMENTS:

❈ 1/2 oz of white rose petals
❈ 16 oz of spring water
❈ Glass bottle for storage

INSTRUCTIONS:

Crush the white rose petals gently, releasing their essence and fragrance.

Place the crushed petals into the spring water, allowing their energy to infuse.

Let the rose petals steep in the water for three days, soaking up the energy of peace and tranquility.

Strain the petals from the water, keeping the liquid pure and infused.

Pour the strained liquid into a glass bottle, sealing it with intention as you chant:

"Petals of white, serene and pure,
Infuse this water with calm so sure.
Tranquility now fill this space,
Bring peace and harmony to every place."

Peaceful Home Blessing

REQUIREMENTS:

❀ Freshly cut parsley
❀ A pan of water

INSTRUCTIONS:

Gather freshly cut parsley and place it in a pan of water.

Let it soak for nine minutes, infusing the water with calming energy.

After the parsley has soaked, take the pan of water and sprinkle it throughout the house.

As you do so, visualize a calm and serene environment, chanting:

"With this water, peace I bring,
Calm and quiet, let it sing.
Throughout this home, tranquility flows,
Harmony and peace in all it shows."

Continue to sprinkle the water until the entire house has been cleansed.

Feel the peace being restored within your home, knowing that serenity now reigns.

You can repeat the Chant of Serenity daily:

"Parsley pure, water bright,
Bring us peace by day and night."

Peaceful Home Pouch

REQUIREMENTS:

❀ Lavender cloth for sewing a small pouch
❀ A small trinket for each household member
❀ Pinches of lavender, rose, and chamomile
❀ A small amethyst
❀ A lavender or pink candle
❀ Peace oil for anointing the candle

INSTRUCTIONS:

Sew a small pouch using the lavender cloth.

Place a small trinket for each household member inside the pouch.

Hold each pinch of lavender, rose, and chamomile for a moment, focusing on your intent for a peaceful home.

Add each pinch to the pouch.

Place a small amethyst inside the pouch.

Anoint the lavender or pink candle with peace oil.

Light the candle and sit in front of it, holding the pouch in your hands.

Whisper the following chant softly three times, focusing on bringing peace to your home:

"Blessed Goddess, most gentle one, Calm my home for me.
Relieve all tension, send it far, So from stress we shall be free.
Touch my family with peace and calm, And the sweetest, softest bliss,
Bless my home, Great Gentle Goddess, With your calming kiss."

Place the pouch beside the candle.

Allow the candle to burn down completely.

Hang the pouch in your home, preferably in the room where everyone gathers the most.

Whenever tension builds, repeat the chant three times.

Envision peace and tranquility radiating from the pouch and the Goddess, filling your home with calm.

Peaceful Home Sprinkle

REQUIREMENTS:

❁ Freshly cut parsley
❁ Pan of water

INSTRUCTIONS:

Find a quiet and serene space to work. Gather fresh parsley and a pan filled with water.

Place the freshly cut parsley into the pan of water.

Allow it to soak for exactly nine minutes, visualizing tranquility and calm spreading through your home.

After nine minutes, take the pan of infused water and slowly walk through each room of your house.

Sprinkle the parsley water lightly around each room, focusing on corners and areas where tension may reside.

As you sprinkle the water, chant with intent:

> "Parsley green, water pure,
> Bring peace and calm, make it sure.
> In every room, in every space,
> Harmony and love now embrace."

Continue to visualize a serene and peaceful environment filling your home.

Feel the calmness settling into every corner, driving away negativity and discord.

When you have finished sprinkling the water throughout your home, return to your starting point.

Take a moment to breathe deeply and affirm the peace and harmony you have brought into your space.

Protecting the House from Evil

REQUIREMENTS:

- ❁ 4 oz. Valerian
- ❁ 2 oz. Rue
- ❁ 2 oz. Bay Leaves
- ❁ 3 tbsp. Dill
- ❁ 2 oz. Caraway
- ❁ 4 parts Lavender
- ❁ 6 tsp. Sandalwood

INSTRUCTIONS:

Begin by gathering all your ingredients and a heat-proof dish or cauldron to burn the incense.

Blend the valerian, rue, bay leaves, dill, caraway, lavender, and sandalwood together, ensuring they are finely ground and mixed well.

As you mix the ingredients, focus your intent on protection and chant:

> "Herbs of power, blend and bind,
> Guard this home with strength divine.
> Evil's touch shall not come near,
> In this space, only love and cheer."

Place a small amount of the mixture onto a burning charcoal disc in your heat-proof dish or cauldron.

Walk through each room of your home, allowing the fragrant smoke to cleanse and protect the space. As you do, repeat:

"By this smoke, protection rise,
Shield this home from prying eyes.
Negative forces, now depart,
Peace and safety fill each part."

Ensure the smoke reaches every corner and doorway, visualizing a barrier of protection forming around your home.

Once you have completed the walkthrough, place the remaining incense mixture in a jar and keep it in a safe place. Use as needed to refresh the protective barrier.

Restore Peace to a Turbulant Home

REQUIREMENTS:

❁ Black candle
❁ Astral candles (one for each person in the home)
❁ Yellow-green candle
❁ Light blue candle
❁ Deity candles (e.g., white and black, or gold and silver)
❁ Incense (frankincense)
❁ White votive candle

INSTRUCTIONS:

Light the Deity candles and the incense.

Sit quietly and meditate on your goal of restoring peace and harmony.

Place the Astral candles approximately 13 inches apart.

Light each Astral candle, saying,

"This flame represents [Name]. As it burns, so does their spirit ignite."

Write down the issues causing unrest in the home.

Discuss these problems openly with everyone involved.

Light the white votive candle, visualizing the start of a peaceful new day.

Light the yellow-green candle, saying:

"All anger and discord now fade away,
Leaving love and joy in their stay.
In our home, let peace take flight,
Bringing harmony day and night."

Meditate for 3-5 minutes, focusing on calming the home's atmosphere.

Burn the list of problems in the flame of the votive candle, visualizing the issues disappearing.

Move the Astral candles closer together.

Light the black candle, saying:

"Negativity now dissolves into air,
Peace and love are everywhere.
Our home is bright, free of strife,
Filled with joy and vibrant life."

Meditate again for 3-5 minutes, imagining the home filled with peace and understanding.

Move the Astral candles even closer.

Light the light blue candle, repeating:
"Our home now is a tranquil place,
Filled with love and gentle grace.
All chaos gone, harmony here,
Peace and calm both far and near."

Hug and kiss each other, expressing joy and relief.

Extinguish the votive candle, followed by the Astral and Deity candles.

Note:

❀ For a more powerful effect, repeat this spell for three consecutive days, using different day candles each time. Allow the Astral candles to touch on the third day.

❀ The ashes of the burned problem paper should be flushed down the toilet to symbolize the removal of negativity from your home.

Room Candle Cleanse

REQUIREMENTS:

❀ White candle
❀ Candle holder
❀ Salt

INSTRUCTIONS:

Place the white candle in its holder at the center of the room you wish to cleanse.

Sprinkle the salt in a clockwise (deosil) circle around the candle, envisioning it creating a barrier against negativity.

Light the candle and focus on its flame. Let your intent for cleansing and protection fill your mind.

With a clear voice, speak these words:

> "Creature of wax and fire's bright,
> Hear my plea, fulfill this rite.
> Cleanse this space, by power of three,
> Remove all negativity.
> With harm to none, this work is done,
> By candle's flame, let peace be won."

Allow the candle to burn for at least one hour, visualizing the light pushing away all negative energies from the room.

After an hour, you may extinguish the candle or let it burn out completely, knowing the room is now cleansed and purified.

Sand Trap to Protect the Home

REQUIREMENTS:

❊ A small glass jar with a close-fitting lid (a clean, recycled spice jar works well)
❊ Equal quantities of two different colors of sand (e.g., fine grayish-white beach sand, yellowish coral sand, orangish desert sand, red volcanic sand, black obsidian sand, etc.)
❊ A spoon
❊ Two small bowls to hold the sands

INSTRUCTIONS:

Thoroughly wash and dry the jar.

Pour one type of sand into the jar until it's just over half filled. Empty this sand into one dish, labeling it "Sand 1."

Clean the jar and repeat with the second type of sand, emptying it into its own dish, labeling it "Sand 2."

Charging the Sand:

Hold your protective hand over "Sand 1." Focus on the sand, visualizing it humming and writhing with protective, projective energy. Touch the sand, envisioning it emitting sparks of bright white light that ensnare negativity and draw it inward. Charge it with your personal power.

Repeat the charging process with "Sand 2."

Creating the Trap:

Place the jar before you.

Scoop out a level spoonful of "Sand 1" and pour it into the jar while saying:

"Sand so fine, a trap you weave,
Banish ill, let none deceive."

Scoop out a level spoonful of "Sand 2" and pour it into the jar while saying:

> "Guard my home, both night and day,
> Keep all harm and bane at bay."

Continue alternating spoonfuls of sand, repeating the respective chants, until the jar is filled.

Close the lid tightly on the jar.

Hold the jar in both hands, visualizing it glowing with protective energy.

Chant:

> "Trap of sand, secure and bright,
> Catch all ill within your light.
> Keep this home from harm and dread,
> By this charm, my will is said."

Place the jar near the main entrance of your home, or in a location where it can work its magic effectively.

Spiritual Barricade, to Lock or Hold Doors Shut

REQUIREMENTS:

❀ Holy water
❀ Salt
❀ Powdered iron

INSTRUCTIONS:

Begin by meditating for at least 15 minutes. Focus your mind on the desired effect of the spell, visualizing the door being firmly locked and impenetrable.

Mix the holy water, salt, and powdered iron together.

Sprinkle the mixture in front of the door you wish to lock.

Place your hands on the door, concentrating your energy. Visualize it flowing down your right arm, through the door, and back into your left arm, creating a continuous circuit.

As you build up power, begin chanting:

"Portal of mine,
with strength combine,
I bind you fast,
your openness past.
Hold firm and tight,
throughout the night,
By power within,
I weave this light."

Continue chanting, imagining the circle of energy moving faster and faster through your arms and the door.

Upon feeling a surge of power, release it with a final visual push, imagining a green field of energy rising up and sealing the door.

Tree Energy Purification for a Household

REQUIREMENTS:

❁ 1 tablespoon dried pine needles
❁ 1 tablespoon dried juniper
❁ 1 tablespoon dried cedar
❁ Self-igniting charcoal

INSTRUCTIONS:

Ensure all ingredients are completely dry.

Grind the pine needles, juniper, and cedar together until they form a fine mixture.

Place the self-igniting charcoal in a fireproof dish.

Light the charcoal and allow it to become fully ignited.

Sprinkle the ground mixture onto the hot charcoal, allowing the incense to fill the air.

As the fragrant smoke rises, move to the center of your home.

Hold the dish and walk to each corner of the room, letting the smoke cleanse and purify the space.

As you move, chant the following incantation:

"Spirits of the corners,
winds of the quarters,
You who stand watching,
and you who hear my voice,
Guard well my home tonight,
ensure all is right.
Purify this space, with nature's embrace,
Let peace and protection now fill this place."

Visualize the smoke carrying away any negative energy, replacing it with a protective and calming presence.

See your home bathed in a glowing, protective light.

Once you have visited each corner, return to the center of your home.

Place the dish safely and allow the incense to burn completely.

Stand for a moment, feeling the purified energy surrounding you.

Warding Off Household Ghosts

REQUIREMENTS:

❀ 3 oz. Juniper Leaves
❀ 4 tbsp. Dried Rosemary
❀ 2 oz. Fennel Seeds
❀ 2 tsp. Basil
❀ 3 tsp. Linden Flowers
❀ 2 tsp. Angelica
❀ Pinch of Salt

INSTRUCTIONS:

Gather all your ingredients and a heat-proof dish or cauldron to burn this incense.

Blend the juniper leaves, dried rosemary, fennel seeds, basil, linden flowers, and angelica together, ensuring they are finely ground and mixed well.

Add a pinch of salt to the mixture for its purifying properties.

As you mix the ingredients, focus on your intent to ward off spirits and chant:

*"Herbs of power, blend and bind,
Keep all spirits from my mind.
Ghosts and phantoms, hear my plea,
Leave this place, let us be."*

Place a small amount of the mixture onto a burning charcoal disc in your heat-proof dish or cauldron.

Walk through each room of your home, allowing the fragrant smoke to cleanse and protect the space. As you do, repeat:

"By this smoke, I cast away,
Spirits lurking, you cannot stay.
Peace and light now fill this place,
Depart from here, leave no trace."

Ensure the smoke reaches every corner and doorway, visualizing a barrier of protection forming around your home.

Once you have completed the walkthrough, place the remaining incense mixture in a jar and keep it in a safe place. Use as needed to refresh the protective barrier.

End the ritual by saying:

"With herbs and smoke, my will is clear,
This home is safe, there's nothing to fear.
Blessed be, this charm shall stay,
Guarding us both night and day."

Welcome Luck into Your Home

REQUIREMENTS:

❁ A green candle
❁ A small bowl of fresh herbs (basil, mint, and rosemary)
❁ A piece of parchment
❁ A quill and green ink
❁ A small charm or talisman (four-leaf clover, horseshoe, etc.)

INSTRUCTIONS:

Cleanse your space and create a sacred circle.

Light the green candle and place it in the center of your altar.

Write the following on the parchment with the quill and green ink:

"Good luck and fortune, hear my plea,
Enter this home and dwell with me.
Abundance flows, blessings pour,
Welcome, luck, through every door."

Place the small bowl of fresh herbs beside the candle.

Hold the charm or talisman in your hands and say:

"Herbs of green and charm of might,
Invite good luck to me this night.
Blessings flow and fill this space,
Good fortune smiles on this place."

Sprinkle a pinch of the herbs around the candle while visualizing luck and abundance entering your home.

74

Hold the parchment over the flame of the green candle and let it burn while saying:

> "This invitation is complete, yet never-ending,
> Good things flow, ever-bending.
> Here and now, and evermore,
> Luck and joy come through my door."

Allow the candle to burn out completely.

Place the charm or talisman near the entrance of your home to continuously invite good luck.

Books by this Author

- The Protection Bible - The Essential Book of Protection Spells and Magic
- The Essential Book of Binding Spells and Magic
- The Essential Book of Cleansing, Blessing, and Purification Spells and Magic
- The Essential Book of Healing Spells and Magic
- The Essential Book of Household Spells and Magic
- The Essential Book of Love Spells and Magic

More Books by Erebus Society

The Standard Book of Candle Magic

by K.P. Theodore

In The Standard Book of Candle Magic you will learn about the use of candles in magical traditions, the meanings of colours so you can create your own candle magic rituals, how to prepare for magical practice, how to cast a standard circle, and over 30 Candle Magic spells for your everyday magical needs.

The Standard Book of Meditation

by K.P. Theodore

Within the pages of this book, you will find a diverse array of meditation techniques waiting to be explored. From breath awareness to body scan, loving-kindness to visualization, the author has meticulously assembled a rich tapestry of practices that invite you to embark on a transformative inner journey.

Wandlore -
A Guide for the Apprentice Wandmaker
by K.P. Theodore

Delve into the ancient and intricate art of wandmaking with this comprehensive guide to the origins, properties, and crafting of magick wands. This book serves as both an introduction to wandlore and a hands-on manual for those who aspire to become skilled wand makers.

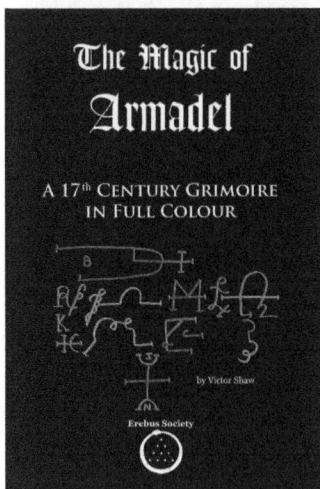

The Magic of Armadel – A 17th Century Grimoire in Full Colour
by Victor Shaw

The Grimoire of Armadel is a book of Celestial Magick and contains information, seals, and sigils of Angels, Demons and other Celestial Spirits.

It is classed as a Christian/Theistic Grimoire, and it was first translated by S.L. McGregor Mathers in the late 1890's from the original French and Latin manuscript that can be found in the Biblotheque l'Arsenal in Paris.

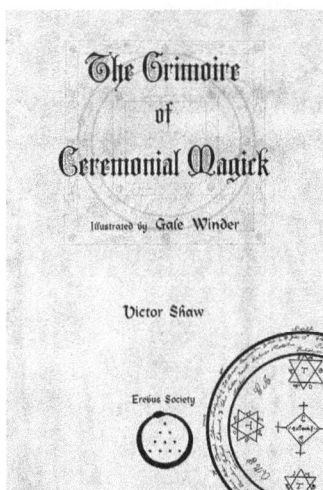

The Grimoire of Ceremonial Magick
by Victor Shaw

This book is a collection of passages, rites, practices, and rituals from various famous Grimoires. It is a cluster of the most obscure and powerful invocations, ceremonies, and pacts, and it explains their history and origins while it refutes certain myths surrounding Ancient Grimoires, and discusses the theology therein.

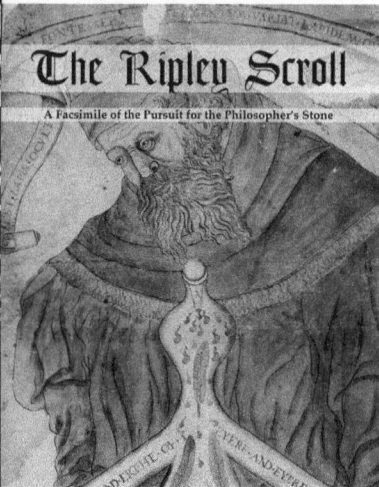

The Ripley Scroll: A Facsimile of the Pursuit for the Philosopher's Stone
by Victor Shaw

The 'Ripley scroll' or 'Ripley Scrowle' is a paramount alchemical work of the 15th century as it depicts the mystical and laborious process for the pursuit of the Philosopher's Stone. A legendary substance that can turn base metals into gold and can also be used in the making of the elixir of life, providing its possessor with prolonged life or even Immortality.

The Fundamental Book of Sigil Magick
by K.P. Theodore

This book serves as a textbook for those who wish to study the art of Sigil Magick. In its pages you will find information about the different kinds of sigils, their use, activation techniques and how to create custom tailored sigils from scratch.

Learn how to captivate emotions, empower the mind, create mental barriers, re-program the brain and alter consciousness by the use of "Mental Sigils".

The Accelerated Necromancer
by Gavin Fox

Necromancy has long been misunderstood, reduced to taboo and superstition. In this insightful work, Gavin redefines the practice, blending witchcraft and chaos magick to offer a responsible, spiritually enriching path.

With practical techniques, seasonal rites, and a fresh take on working with the dead, this book is a must-read for those seeking to walk the shadows with wisdom and reverence.

www.ingramcontent.com/pod-product-compliance
Lightning Source LLC
Chambersburg PA
CBHW032026040426
42448CB00006B/739